Woodbridge Town Library

W9-CDS-145

A2180 157218 7

1/03

Donated by

Friends of
The Woodbridge
Library

© DEMCO, INC. 1990 PRINTED IN U.S.A.

DATE DUE

OVERDUE FINE
$0.10 PER DAY

DEMCO

100 GREAT SALAD DRESSINGS

100
GREAT SALAD
DRESSINGS

SALLY GRIFFITHS

PHOTOGRAPHS BY
SIMON WHEELER

WOODBRIDGE TOWN LIBRARY
10 NEWTON ROAD
WOODBRIDGE, CT 08525

CASSELLPAPERBACKS

Text © Sally Griffiths, 1994

Photographs © George Weidenfeld & Nicolson, 1994

Sally Griffiths has asserted her right to be identified
as the Author of this Work

This paperback edition first published in 2002 by
Cassell Paperbacks, Cassell & Co, Wellington House,
125 Strand, London, WC2R 0BB

First published in the United Kingdom in 1994 by
George Weidenfeld & Nicolson Limited

All rights reserved. No part of this publication may be reproduced
in any material form (including photocopying or storing it in any
medium by electronic means and whether or not transiently or
incidentally to some other use of this publication) without the
written permission of the copyright owner, except in accordance
with the provisions of the Copyright,

A CIP catalogue record for this book is available from
the British Library
ISBN 1-84188-169-4

Designed by Thumb Design Limited

Printed and bound in Italy

CONTENTS

ACKNOWLEDGEMENTS

I would like to thank my publisher Michael Dover for giving me the opportunity to write this book and for holding my hand throughout the project. I am also indebted to Suzannah Gough, my wonderful managing editor whose enthusiasm and energy throughout the assignment have been inspirational.

I am deeply grateful to Gillian Haslam, my long-suffering editor who has the patience of Job. Her remarkable organization and delightful easy-going manner has enabled me to give of my best. To Simon Wheeler whose splendid photographs make the book a visual delight, and whose company made the project so enjoyable. I would like to thank Ian Pape and Tony Seddon of Thumb Design Partnership for creating brilliant designs which complement the photographs and the text of the book to perfection.

In particular I am indebted to Simon Lowe, Andrew Leaman and Howard Malin, joint owners of the Feathers Hotel, for their continued support and extraordinary generosity throughout the project. To Tom Lewis, the efficient manager of the Feathers Hotel who, together with his delightful staff, made my frequent visits to the hotel, and our stay during photography, so enjoyable.

I would especially like to thank Mark Lake of Taylor and Lake who most generously provided all the oils, vinegars, seasonings and pastes for the photographs.

Last but not least, I would like to thank my friend and collaborator David Lewis for his inspirational contribution to the book. If it hadn't been for his invaluable guidance I might still be floundering around amongst the sauce boats – Royal Worcester of course!

INTRODUCTION

I have never believed that to enjoy motoring one has to be a Grand Prix winner or that to enjoy boating one must have been one of the first three in the Whitbread Round-the-World Race.

On more or less the same terms, I see no reason against writing books about cookery even if one wasn't born a five-star chef. Quite simply, I have a passion for good cooking, whether it be a simple snack or a wickedly elaborate gourmet dinner.

Like most enthusiasts, I enjoy passing on my discoveries to those also interested in cooking. Inevitably, then, when I was asked to write about salad dressings, I thought, why not? After all, precious little has been written about this subject, although hundreds of cooks want to know more about these simple finishing touches to successful cooking.

But any enthusiasm verging on passion needs sound technical back-up. Happily I knew exactly where to go, for during one of my assignments for *House & Garden* magazine, I had met David Lewis, head chef at the Feathers Hotel in Woodstock, Oxfordshire. His confident expertise and lively, innovative style greatly impressed me right from my first experiences of his culinary skills. I knew immediately that David was the right man to provide the recipes, not just because he is destined to be numbered amongst the limited group of master chefs, but already, at the ripe old age of twenty-five, he possesses that rarest of all qualities in a great cook: he is ready and willing to pass on his knowledge. So David and I became partners in this venture. I believe the following pages show that process in action.

Since oils, vinegars and seasonings are the basic ingredients of any salad dressing, several pages are dedicated to the importance of their numerous roles, along with other relevant information. I also felt it would be helpful to list a few useful utensils as well as some basic ingredients for the storecupboard. The remainder of the book is dedicated to the recipes themselves, including over 100 dressings and mayonnaises.

For every recipe, David has listed several appropriate ingredients or dishes to complement the dressing. However, these are intended merely as guidelines as it would be impossible to list all the variations – the secret is to experiment. (A cross-index at the back of the book has been specially compiled to give the reader easy access to hundreds of different and exciting combinations.)

It has given me enormous pleasure to work with David and to learn so much about this fascinating subject. I hope you have as much enjoyment reading and using this book as I have had writing it.

UTENSILS

This is a complete list of the utensils used for the recipes in this book. Many are everyday items kept in the kitchen anyway, so it is unnecessary to stock up with even more expensive equipment. However, certain utensils, such as an oil pourer, liquidiser and blender, are good investments because they save time, and in doing so, make the recipes easier to follow and more fun.

Rock salt and black pepper mills Salt and pepper are used in most of the recipes so it is worth investing in good grinders.

Chopping board A wooden chopping board prevents the work surface being damaged by sharp knives.

Collection of screw-top jars Just the job for shaking ingredients and keeping salad dressings in.

Garlic crusher Try to find one which empties the pulp easily as they are less messy.

Hand or battery-operated whisk An invaluable piece of equipment used in many of the recipes.

Knives Make sure they are sufficiently sharp to cope with extra-fine slicing and chopping.

Lemon squeezer Buy one with a guard to prevent the pips falling into the dressing.

Liquidiser or blender Either or both will *definitely* save time, energy and effort!

Measuring jug Buy a jug which indicates metric and imperial measurements clearly.

Special oil pourer or a long, slim funnel connected to a cork which fits into the neck of the bottle – a must in any kitchen and invaluable when making mayonnaise. Obtainable from a good kitchen shop.

Pestle and mortar A quick and easy way to crush a small amount of herbs, spices, garlic, black peppercorns or rock salt, for example, allowing the full flavour of the ingredient to be released.

Plastic chopping board Use it to chop garlic and any ingredient that stains or has a strong smell.

Selection of bowls A variety of shapes and sizes is always useful for mixing ingredients.

Salad bowl There's a wonderful selection available, ranging from wood to brightly coloured ceramics and glass. Don't buy anything too small – it's maddening when tossing the salad and the leaves keep falling out.

Spatula A useful implement; just the job for scraping the last drops of mayonnaise out of the bowl!

Wooden spoons They are less abrasive than metal spoons.

THE STORECUPBOARD

Many of the ingredients used in these recipes form part of the everyday storecupboard.
There are others which are an extravagance to keep just on the off-chance they might
be needed; some which deteriorate quickly and many that are best fresh anyway. The
following list of ingredients has been specially compiled so that at least fifty recipes
can be made without a trip to the shops!

Oil
Store in a cool, dark place.
Olive oil, walnut oil, sesame oil, sunflower oil

Vinegar
Keep tightly sealed, away from the light.
White wine vinegar, red wine vinegar, balsamic vinegar,
rice vinegar

Mustard
Mustard will last longer in the fridge.
English mustard, Dijon mustard, grain mustard, green
herb mustard

Salt and Pepper
*Store whole black peppercorns in a dry place. Salt does
not require airtight storage but it does absorb water –
mix with a few grains of rice to keep it dry.*
Black peppercorns, green peppercorns, rock salt,
table salt

Paste
*Paste will last indefinitely as long as the
pots are not opened. Once open, cover and
use as quickly as possible.*
Green olive paste, black olive paste,
chilli paste, red pepper paste, horseradish
paste, curry paste, tapenade

Sauces
Keep out of direct sunlight.
Soya sauce, tabasco sauce, pesto sauce, oyster sauce,
Angostura bitters

Nuts and Seeds
Once the packet has been opened, store in an airtight container.
Flaked almonds, pine kernels, walnuts, poppy seeds, sesame seeds,
caraway seeds

General Ingredients
Lime pickle, curry powder, small tin of anchovy fillets, small jar of
black olives, small jar of green olives, small jar of capers, jar of
small gherkins, horseradish relish, tin or jar of red peppers, clear
honey, muscovado sugar, redcurrant jelly

In the Fridge
Plain yoghurt, fromage frais or crème fraîche, eggs

Fruit and Vegetable Bowl
Limes, lemons, oranges, garlic, shallots,
red chilli

Window Box Selection
Tarragon, chives, parsley, mint, dill,
basil, chervil, coriander

OILS

Good quality oil has the most wonderful taste in the world and is one of the
most important ingredients for mayonnaise and salad dressings. The best way to learn
about oil is to experiment and sample oils from different countries, for example
Greece, France, Spain and Italy. Each oil not only looks and tastes different
but has its own individual character.

Where did olive oil originate? Olive oil came from Asia Minor and the Mediterranean. The olive tree was known to be cultivated in Syria and Palestine in 3000 BC.

What does extra virgin oil mean? It is the best quality olive oil produced from the 'first pressing'. This is a method where fresh ripe olives are 'cold-pressed' (i.e. lightly pressed) to extract the very best oil. The taste of extra virgin oil is subtle and fruity and the colour ranges from pale yellow to green.

When is extra virgin olive oil used? It is used primarily to add a wonderful fruity taste and aroma to salad dressings. However, in the Mediterranean region olive oil often takes the place of butter.

Does olive oil have any nutritional value? It is high in mono-unsaturated fats and it has been proved that where there is a high consumption of olive oil, there is a low incidence of heart disease.

What is the best way to store olive oil? Store the oil in a cool, dark place, preferably out of the sun.

How to recognise oil that is 'off'? It has a distinct rancid smell. Olive oil will keep in a cool, dark place for 2–3 years but once opened use within 1 or 2 months. Walnut oil is best kept in the refrigerator as it deteriorates more quickly.

If you store olive oil in the fridge, it can solidify or turn cloudy. Can this be rectified? Either leave the bottle in a warm room or run it under the hot tap and it will soon clear. This process will not affect the taste or the quality of the oil.

Why are some olive oils greener or darker than others? The colour of the oil is affected by the soil and the climate of the area in which it grows. Green oil goes yellow with age.

Where do the strongest flavoured olive oils come from? They tend to come from the hottest regions of the Mediterranean.

Is there a good time to buy olive oil? In the Mediterranean olive oil is produced between December and February. As a general rule there is no reference to the year it is bottled; however, some small estates put the date on the label.

Which is the best way to choose an olive oil? Experiment – it is the only way to discover and learn about the various tastes. As with wine, the price and the name on the label are indicative of the quality. Cheap olive oil has little flavour; try sunflower oil instead.

Which is the best olive oil to use for salad dressings? Extra virgin olive oil – buy it in large cans, it's far more economical.

How to make flavoured olive oil? Herbs and spices can be added to flavour oil. Left in the bottle, they look very decorative.

What is the advantage of using flavoured oils? They provide a quick method of adding a particular taste to dressings.

How to make garlic flavoured oil? Add four or five garlic cloves to 1 litre (1¾ pint) of olive oil.

When are vegetable, sunflower or groundnut oils used in a dressing? Other oils are used in a salad dressing when price is a consideration. Alternatively, it can be a matter of taste.

Why are some oils so expensive to buy? One factor is the time it takes to pick the olives. They are harvested in the winter and usually picked by hand. Each tree produces around 8 kg (18 1b) of olives and it takes 5kg (11 lb) of olives to make 1 litre (1¾ pint) of oil, so it is a painstaking affair.

VINEGARS

There are many different types of vinegar, each with its own individual strength,
flavour and quality. Vinegar is one of the most important ingredients in a dressing and
should be used with respect, otherwise it can overwhelm the flavour of a salad.

What does the word vinegar mean? It means 'sour wine'. The term derives from the French *vin aigre*.

Where did vinegar originate? In the wine-growing areas of the Mediterranean. In all probability, vinegar was discovered by accident when wine was left in the hot sun and went sour. It was originally used for cleaning metals and for preserving fruits and vegetables.

How is vinegar made? By subjecting alcohol to heat, air and bacteria.

Where does wine vinegar come from? Some of the best wine vinegars come from France.

When is white wine vinegar used? It is almost always used in recipes requiring wine vinegar.

When is red wine vinegar used? When a stronger flavour is required, as red is stronger than white.

How long does vinegar keep and how should it be stored? Vinegar will keep for several years although it starts to lose freshness and colour with age – this applies particularly to herb or fruit flavoured vinegars. Store in an airtight container, away from the light.

How can you tell the quality of vinegar? Quite simply by the taste and the price!

What is balsamic vinegar, and where does it come from? For centuries balsamic vinegar was the well-kept secret of Modena in Italy, and was only produced commercially in 1966. It has a thick, rich, dark-brown appearance and is fruity and sweet. However, balsamic vinegar should be used sparingly because it is very strong. Good balsamic vinegar is expensive – beware of cheaper varieties as these are often diluted with an inferior quality vinegar to lower the price.

How many different types of vinegar are there? The main vinegars are wine vinegar, grain vinegar and rice vinegar.

When is malt vinegar used? Use it with fish and chips or for pickling, but not in a dressing because it is far too strong. Malt vinegar is naturally colourless; colour is achieved by adding caramel.

What effect will flavoured vinegar have on a salad dressing? It will enhance the salad by flavouring it with the taste of the herb or fruit used in the vinegar.

Which vinegar goes best with which oil? Any good quality vinegar goes well with a good quality olive oil.

How to make herb-flavoured vinegar? Add a few sprigs of fresh herbs to white wine vinegar and leave for several weeks – the time can vary so keep tasting. Strain into clean containers and seal tightly. Leave the herbs in the bottle for a pleasing visual effect.

Can you use dried herbs to flavour vinegar? They can be used, but the taste is inferior compared with fresh herbs.

Can fresh fruit be used to flavour vinegar? Yes, strong tasting fruits such as raspberries produce the best flavours.

How to make fruit flavoured vinegar? Use white wine vinegar with fresh ripe fruit. For example, combine 500g (1lb 1½oz) raspberries with 1.25 litres (2¼ pints) white wine vinegar. Place in clean jars and leave to steep in a warm place for several weeks. Shake the jars occasionally. Then strain the mixture or, alternatively, leave the fruit in the vinegar. Pour into clean bottles, label and seal.

What flavoured vinegars are available commercially? The list is endless but here are some examples: tarragon, garlic, dill, herb, mint, rosemary, lemon, peach, raspberry, blueberry, blackberry and redcurrant.

SEASONINGS

MUSTARD is a hot spice which derives from the cabbage family. Black and brown mustard plants produce small round seeds that have a strong flavour, whilst white mustard, which has large yellow seeds and is more commonly seen in Mediterranean areas, is far less pungent.

When was mustard first used? It probably first graced the tables of the ancient Egyptians in 2000 BC. Pope John XXII employed a cousin from Dijon as his personal *moutardier* in 1316, and during the eighteenth and nineteenth centuries mustard became very fashionable with about a hundred different varieties available for consumption.

How is mustard made? Mustard is made by a simple process which entails soaking the grains and then grinding them into a paste. If a smooth mustard is required, the husks are removed, then salt and vinegar are added to flavour and preserve the paste.

How best to store mustard? Both dry and prepared mustard will keep unopened for about two years. Once opened, put prepared mustard in the refrigerator and dry mustard in a dark, dry place.

Why are some prepared mustards bright yellow? This is due to the addition of turmeric, often used to give flavour and colour.

What are the different strengths of mustard? Basically, all mustards are one strength, but some are extra hot.

What is flavoured mustard? It is mustard flavoured with either strong herbs or spices and there are hundreds of different varieties available in supermarkets and delicatessens.

What effect does mustard have on a salad dressing? Apart from adding flavour, mustard is an emulsifier. It stabilizes mayonnaise, and in a salad dressing it holds the oil and vinegar together.

How many different varieties of mustard are available today ? Probably thousands! Amongst the most popular are: American mustard – *bright yellow and sweet*, Bordeaux mustard – *mild*, Dijon mustard – *strong, but milder than English mustard*, English mustard – *mild or very strong*, German mustard – *dark and mild*, Moutarde de Meaux – *mild, wholegrain mustard*.

SALT was once valued so highly that it was used as an offering to God. Today it is a relatively cheap commodity and its role is decidedly more practical. Salt is used to season and preserve food, but it also acts as a precious nutrient to the body.

Where does salt come from? It comes either from the sea, where it is obtained by evaporation in salt pans, or it is excavated from mines and then purified for use.

What is salt? Salt is a preservative and can be used in a dry state or mixed with water to make brine. There are two varieties of salt: rock salt and sea salt.

Which is the best salt to use in salad dressings? This is a personal choice but many people believe rock salt is the best because it has a good, pure flavour.

Why do we use salt in cooking? Salt has an affinity with water and brings out the flavour of the food.

Which is the best way to store salt? Store in a warm, dry place. To prevent dampness, mix a few grains of rice with the salt.

Which salt has the best flavour? It is said that untreated rock salt, which is produced all over the world, has the best flavour.

What is table salt? It is finely ground rock or sea salt.

How can too much salt in a dressing be rectified? Adjust with lemon juice, vinegar or sugar. Add a small amount at a time.

What is sel gris? It is a coarse grey salt used mainly in France.

What is unrefined salt? It is a product not dissimilar to sel gris and is grey/black in colour. It should be ground in a pestle and mortar and is quite often damp when sold.

Is it best to buy expensive, finely packaged salt? No, although Maldon salt is excellent and has a lovely 'salty' taste.

Which is the strongest, sea or rock salt? Sea salt is definitely more powerful than rock salt, so use less.

PEPPER, the king of spices, was at one time worth its weight in gold. It comes from the plant *Piper Nigrum* and today accounts for one-quarter of the world's spice trade, India being the foremost producer.

When was pepper first recorded? Around the fourth century BC. Its Sanskrit name was *Pippali*.

How does pepper grow? Black or white pepper is the dried fruit of a tropical vine, native to India.

Which is the best way to store peppercorns? Store dried peppercorns in an airtight container in a cool, dark place. The same applies to ground pepper, but the keeping time is shorter.

What are green peppercorns? These are unripe, fresh berries which are preserved in bottles or cans.

Why are some peppercorns black? They are unripe green peppercorns which are left to ferment for a few days before being sun-dried.

Why are black peppercorns so popular? Freshly milled black peppercorns emit a wonderful aromatic fragrance which immediately enhances the flavour of food.

What are white peppercorns? They come from ripe red berries which, after harvesting, are soaked in water to remove the outer skin. Not as strong as black pepper, white pepper is generally used to complement light-coloured foods.

How many different types of peppercorn are there? There is actually only one pepper berry. The strength and flavour varies depending where the plants are grown and the drying method.

How to rectify an over-peppered dressing? This is a difficult one; if it really is awful, nothing can be done so throw the mixture away and start again. Otherwise, adjust it with sugar or honey, depending on the flavour of the basic ingredients.

What is the advantage of using ground pepper? None whatsoever unless a pepper mill is unavailable.

How to crush peppercorns? In a pestle and mortar. Alternatively, put them in into a strong polythene bag and crush with a rolling pin.

PASTES are an innovative, labour-saving way of buying strong, concentrated flavourings. One spoonful is usually enough to add sufficient extra taste to a dressing or mayonnaise.

What is a paste and when is it used? It is a vegetable, fruit, fish or meat purée, which can be used to add flavour.

How long can a paste be stored? It will keep indefinitely but once the jar or tin has been opened, store it in the refrigerator. To prevent air from reaching the paste, cover the surface with either olive or sunflower oil and it will keep for several years.

Where do pastes come from? The raw ingredients come from all over the world. However, many wonderful pastes such as artichoke, sun-dried tomato, mushroom and aubergine are made in the Mediterranean area.

Which is the most popular flavour? There is a wonderful variety of pastes available in supermarkets and delicatessens. Green or black olive paste is probably the most popular. Ideally olive paste should be made from just one variety of olive to distinguish the type.

19

THE RECIPES

CLASSIC MAYONNAISE

This is the basic recipe and makes 300ml (10 fl oz/1¼ cups) of mayonnaise which is sufficient for 4 to 6 people.

2 egg yolks, size 2
1-2 tablespoons white wine vinegar
1 teaspoon grain mustard
300ml (10 fl oz/1¼ cups) olive oil–light (strong olive oil, i.e. extra virgin, can make mayonnaise taste bitter)
Juice of ½ lemon
Salt and pepper

*Beat egg yolks, white wine vinegar and mustard in a bowl until almost white. Add oil **drop by drop**, beating continuously until about half the oil has been used. Add the rest of the oil in a very slow stream, still beating constantly. When all the the oil has been incorporated into the mixture, season with lemon juice, salt and pepper.*

QUICK MAYONNAISE

1 whole egg, size 3
1 tablespoon white wine vinegar
1 teaspoon grain mustard
175ml (6 fl oz/¾ cup) olive oil – light
175ml (6 fl oz/¾ cup) sunflower oil
Juice of ½ lemon
Salt and pepper

Put egg, white wine vinegar and mustard into a blender and mix together until creamy and smooth. With the motor still running, add the oils in a slow, steady stream. Season with lemon juice, salt and pepper.
• Use a light olive oil for this dressing; heavy, strong-flavoured oils (including extra virgin olive oil) can produce mayonnaise with a bitter taste.

USEFUL TIPS

*• If the mixture starts to curdle, **don't panic!** Put **another** egg yolk into **a separate bowl** and beating constantly, add the curdled mixture to it **drop by drop**. Then continue with the recipe.*
*• Make sure **all** the ingredients are at room temperature. Leave them out 3-4 hours before making the mayonnaise – this will help prevent curdling.*
• If the consistency of the mixture gets too thick, add water – one teaspoon at a time – until it corrects itself.
• To thicken mayonnaise, slowly add more oil until the correct consistency is achieved.

• Plain or flavoured mayonnaise can be thinned down and used as a dressing for salads. Add 300ml (10 fl oz/1¼ cups) cold water to basic mayonnaise and mix together well. Alternatively, it may be more appropriate to use half the quantity of mayonnaise in which case add 150ml (5 fl oz/⅔ cup) water.
• Mayonnaise can be kept for 48 hours in an airtight container in the refrigerator.
• A more economical way to make good mayonnaise is to use a combination of sunflower and olive oil.

Left Bowl of 'basic recipe' mayonnaise

FLAVOURING MAYONNAISE

FLAVOURED OILS

One way to vary the flavour of mayonnaise is to use a flavoured oil, for example, walnut, hazelnut, basil, tomato, lobster or rosemary oil. Using the basic recipe mayonnaise (page 23) substitute 300ml (10 fl oz/1¼ cups) olive oil with the following combination instead: 250ml (8 fl oz/1 cup) olive oil and 50ml (2 fl oz/¼ cup) flavoured oil. Certain flavoured oils such as sesame and pistachio are very strong so less is needed.

PASTES, HERBS AND VEGETABLES

Another way to alter the flavour of plain mayonnaise is to combine it with a ready-made paste or a solid ingredient such as a vegetable or herb. Each of the following recipes contains the full quantity of basic recipe mayonnaise (page 23). To make less use half the quantity of **all** the ingredients.

Hot chilli mayonnaise *Delicious with chargrilled food.*
Take 2 teaspoons of chilli paste and mix thoroughly with the mayonnaise. For a milder flavour, use 1 teaspoon of chilli paste.

Sun-dried tomato mayonnaise *The pungent flavour of sun-dried tomatoes complements goat's cheese, forest mushrooms and pasta beautifully.*
Take 2 teaspoons of sun-dried tomato paste and mix thoroughly with the mayonnaise. Season to taste.

Basil mayonnaise *A wonderful summer combination, perfect with mussels, squid, shellfish, rice and ham.*
Take 1 tablespoon of basil paste and mix thoroughly with the mayonnaise. Season with salt and pepper. For extra flavour, mix in four large, fresh basil leaves, finely chopped.

Horseradish mayonnaise *Guaranteed to spice up left-over roast beef, this dressing has a gutsy flavour which also enhances more subtle flavours such as ham, salmon, smoked salmon or herrings.*
Take 2 tablespoons of horseradish relish and mix thoroughly with the mayonnaise. Season with salt and pepper.

Beetroot mayonnaise *This colourful mayonnaise looks marvellous against paler ingredients such as baked cod or crab.*
Take 50g (2 oz/¼ cup) beetroot or one small beetroot, cooked and finely grated, and mix thoroughly with the mayonnaise. Season with salt and pepper to taste.

Black bean and oyster sauce mayonnaise *A richly flavoured mayonnaise which is out of this world with chargrilled tuna or fish kebabs.*
Take 1 tablespoon of black bean sauce and 1 tablespoon of oyster sauce, mix thoroughly with the mayonnaise and season.

Grain mustard mayonnaise *This mayonnaise is the perfect choice to serve with baked cheese, grilled chicken, celery or avocado. Alternatively, it makes a wonderful dip.*
Take 2 tablespoons of grain mustard, mix thoroughly with the mayonnaise and season to taste.

Celeriac mayonnaise *The delicate flavour of celeriac is accentuated when it accompanies baked ham, cold poached salmon, beef, venison, hare or chargrilled chicken.*
Take 100g (4 oz/½ cup) celeriac, cooked and finely grated, and mix thoroughly with the mayonnaise. Season to taste.

Asparagus mayonnaise *This mayonnaise has a delicate taste which complements other subtle flavours such as smoked trout or asparagus and smoked salmon to perfection.*
Take 100g (4 oz/½ cup) asparagus, cooked and finely chopped, and mix thoroughly with the mayonnaise. Season with salt and pepper.

Curry mayonnaise *This versatile dressing can be hot and spicy, or creamy and mild depending on the dish it is to accompany. Try it with salmon, turkey and chicken or potatoes and beef.*
Take 1 tablespoon of curry paste and mix thoroughly with the mayonnaise. Season with salt and pepper to taste. Use less curry paste for a milder flavour. Try tikka, tandoori or satay paste in place of curry paste.

For each of the following recipes use the full quantity
of basic recipe mayonnaise (page 23).

SAFFRON MAYONNAISE

This delicately flavoured mayonnaise goes beautifully with smoked salmon, poached or grilled fish, new potatoes and haricot beans.

Mayonnaise (basic recipe)
½ teaspoon saffron powder or threads
150ml (5fl oz/⅔ cup) dry vermouth

Put saffron and vermouth into a heavy saucepan and reduce over a medium heat until two-thirds of the liquid has evaporated. Remove from heat and when cool, mix thoroughly with the mayonnaise. Season with salt and pepper if necessary.

SOYA AND GINGER MAYONNAISE

This mouthwatering recipe has a strong oriental flavour. Delicious with duck, goose, cauliflower, bean sprouts, white beans or brown rice.

Mayonnaise (basic recipe)
150ml (5fl oz/⅔ cup) soya sauce
25g (1 oz/2 tablespoons) candied stem ginger, finely chopped
150ml (5fl oz/⅔ cup) clear honey
1 shallot, finely chopped
1 clove garlic, crushed
85ml (3 fl oz/⅓ cup) balsamic vinegar

Place all the ingredients except the mayonnaise in a heavy saucepan, and slowly reduce the liquid over a low heat until three-quarters of it has evaporated. Remove from the heat and, when cool, purée the mixture in a liquidiser. Pour into a bowl and stir in the mayonnaise. Season with salt and pepper.
•For a more delicate flavour, use half the purée with the full quantity of mayonnaise.

Left A variety of flavoured mayonnaises including caviar and dill, saffron, soya and ginger, pesto, and smoked bacon and tarragon

PESTO MAYONNAISE

An all-time favourite, this aromatic mayonnaise is simply bursting with flavour. Serve with prawns (shrimp), scallops, smoked wild boar, smoked goose or chargrilled vegetables.

Mayonnaise (basic recipe)

1 tablespoon pesto sauce

Juice of ½ lemon

Blend pesto sauce and lemon juice, then add to the mayonnaise and mix together well. Season with salt and pepper to taste.

CORIANDER AND LIME MAYONNAISE

This aromatic sauce is simple to make and tastes wonderful with halibut, scallops, trout and mussels.

Mayonnaise (basic recipe)

25g (1 oz/2 tablespoons) fresh coriander, chopped

Rind of 2 limes, grated

Juice of 2 limes

Put all the ingredients in a bowl and stir thoroughly. Season with salt and pepper to taste.

CAVIAR AND DILL MAYONNAISE

This is sheer extravagance, and perfectly wonderful with lobster, scampi, steamed or baked fish, and cucumber.

Mayonnaise (basic recipe)

25g (1 oz/2 tablespoons) fresh dill, chopped

50g (2 oz/¼ cup) caviar

Juice of ½ lemon

Put all the ingredients in a bowl and stir until well blended. Season with salt and pepper to taste.

SWEET PEPPER AND RED CHILLI MAYONNAISE

Wickedly moreish, this pungent mayonnaise is wonderful with chargrilled vegetables such as artichokes, peppers and aubergines (eggplant) or chargrilled steaks, prawns (shrimp) and sausages.

Mayonnaise (basic recipe)

50g (2 oz/¼ cup) red pepper, finely chopped

2 red chilli peppers, very finely sliced

1 teaspoon garlic, crushed

½ teaspoon tabasco sauce

Put all the ingredients in a bowl and mix together well. If necessary, season with salt and pepper.

GRAIN MUSTARD AND TARRAGON MAYONNAISE

The subtle flavour of this refreshing mayonnaise goes beautifully with chicken, guinea fowl, tomatoes, ham and broad (lima) beans.

Mayonnaise (basic recipe)

25g (1 oz/2 tablespoons) fresh tarragon, chopped

2 tablespoons grain mustard

Put all the ingredients in a bowl and stir until well mixed. Season with salt and pepper.

GARLIC MAYONNAISE (Aïoli Sauce)

This versatile sauce is a great favourite and widely used in the south of France. Its wonderful garlicky flavour is delicious with pasta, chicken, beef, roast peppers, clams and shellfish.

2 hard-boiled egg yolks, sieved

1 egg yolk, size 2

4 cloves garlic, crushed

300ml (10 fl oz/1¼ cups) olive oil

Juice of ½ lemon

1-2 teaspoons water

Salt and pepper

*Cream cooked eggs and raw yolk with the garlic, then add the water to make a smooth paste. Add olive oil **drop by drop** whisking all the time. Season with salt, pepper and lemon juice.*

SPINACH AND NUTMEG MAYONNAISE

This is a wonderful combination which complements plain, delicate ingredients such as lentils, cheese, leeks, ham or potatoes to perfection.

Mayonnaise (basic recipe)

100g (4 oz/½ cup) spinach leaves, cooked and puréed

½ teaspoon grated nutmeg

Juice of ½ lemon

Put all the ingredients in a bowl and stir until well blended. Season with salt and pepper.

TARTAR MAYONNAISE

A tasty dressing especially designed to complement the more delicate flavour of fish cakes, tuna, fried fish, mushrooms and potatoes.

25g (1 oz/2 tablespoons) capers, finely chopped

25g (1 oz/2 tablespoons) gherkins (cornichons), finely chopped

1 shallot, finely chopped

25g (1 oz/2 tablespoons) fresh parsley, chopped

Juice of ½ lemon

Put all the ingredients in a bowl and stir together well. Season with salt and pepper.

SMOKED BACON AND TARRAGON MAYONNAISE

An ingenious combination which can be used in a hundred different ways! Try it with tomatoes, cheese, haricot beans or lentils, for example.

Mayonnaise (basic recipe)

100g (4 oz/½ cup) smoked streaky bacon, fried and cut into thin strips

15g (½ oz/1 tablespoon) fresh tarragon, chopped

Place all the ingredients in a bowl and mix together well. If necessary, season with salt and pepper.

Potato salad using plain mayonnaise

ANCHOVY MAYONNAISE

Generally associated with fish, this versatile mayonnaise is also delicious served with poached or boiled eggs, vegetable flans, veal, chargrilled sardines, or smoked beef.

Mayonnaise (basic recipe)

100g (4 oz/½ cup) anchovy fillets, finely chopped

Juice of ½ lemon

Put all the ingredients in a bowl and mix together really well. Season with salt and pepper to taste.

WATERCRESS MAYONNAISE

This colourful dressing is a knockout!. Serve with beef, salmon, bresaola (dried beef), trout and herrings.

Mayonnaise (basic recipe)

50g (2 oz/¼ cup) or one bunch watercress, finely chopped

Put the ingredients in a bowl and stir until evenly blended. Season with salt and pepper to taste.

CLASSIC VINAIGRETTE

This is the basic recipe for plain vinaigrette. It is the most widely used dressing and can be used to flavour any kind of salad.

4 tablespoons olive oil
1 tablespoon white wine vinegar
1 teaspoon Dijon mustard
Salt and pepper

Place all the ingredients in a screw-top jar and shake vigorously. Season with salt and pepper to taste.

USEFUL TIPS

• *Unless otherwise specified, always use extra virgin olive oil for dressings.*
• *Plain vinaigrette is best made fresh but can be kept for 2 or 3 days in an airtight container in the refrigerator.*
• *For a more garlicky flavour, add ½ clove of crushed garlic to plain vinaigrette and whisk well.*
• *Use red wine vinegar in place of white wine vinegar to alter the colour and the strength of a dressing.*
• *A quick way to alter the taste of plain vinaigrette is to use olive oil or vinegar infused with spices or herbs. These are available in most delicatessens and supermarkets but can also be made at home, (see pages 15 and 16).*
• *Nut oils such as walnut or hazelnut make a delicious alternative to plain vinaigrette. Substitute 4 tablespoons of olive oil with 2 tablespoons olive oil and 2 tablespoons nut oil.*

Another way to vary the flavour of a plain vinaigrette is to substitute **one** of the basic ingredients with another flavour. Take **tarragon** for example:
• Tarragon vinegar in place of white wine vinegar, or
• Tarragon mustard instead of Dijon mustard, or
• Tarragon-flavoured oil in place of olive oil.

For a stronger flavour substitute **two** of the ingredients. For example:
• Tarragon vinegar and tarragon mustard in place of white wine vinegar and Dijon mustard, or
• Tarragon-flavoured oil and tarragon mustard instead of olive oil and Dijon mustard, or
• Tarragon-flavoured oil and tarragon vinegar in lieu of olive oil and white wine vinegar.

An extra strong flavour is acquired by substituting **all** the ingredients (except salt and pepper) for an alternative flavour. However, be careful as certain flavours are stronger than others and by using all of them at once the mixture can become overpowering. It all boils down to individual taste, so keep experimenting!

There is a wide variety of different flavoured oils, vinegars and mustards to choose from. Look in supermarkets, specialist food shops and delicatessens; between them they stock almost every available flavour. The trick is to experiment because at the end of the day it comes down to personal taste.

Here are a few examples of interesting flavours to watch out for:
basil, cider, lemon, paprika, chilli, rosemary, hazelnut, walnut, sesame, almond, pistachio, truffle, raspberry, mint, garlic, dill, sage, thyme, shallot and cherry.

Left Bowl of vinaigrette dressing

WALNUT AND RASPBERRY DRESSING

A slightly sharp, fruity dressing, delicious with a mixed salad, avocado, chicken or cheese.

4 ripe, fresh raspberries, squashed to a pulp

15g (½ oz/1 tablespoon) walnuts, chopped

8 tablespoons walnut oil

2 tablespoons raspberry vinegar

Place all the ingredients in a screw-top jar and shake vigorously until well combined. Season with salt and pepper to taste.

FROMAGE FRAIS AND TAPENADE DRESSING

Try this lovely dark, creamy dressing with fresh tuna, salmon, sea bass, roasted aubergines (eggplant) or pasta.

300ml (10 fl oz/1¼ cups) fromage frais

100g (4 oz/½ cup) stoned black olives

8 anchovy fillets, drained and rinsed

1 tablespoons capers, drained

4 tablespoons olive oil

Rind and juice of 1 lemon

½ teaspoon Dijon mustard

Place all the ingredients except the fromage frais in a blender and mix until a rough paste is formed. Transfer the mixture to a bowl and gently fold in the fromage frais.

• *For a thinner consistency, add 4 tablespoons water.*

HAZELNUT AND SHERRY DRESSING

A strong, evocative dressing that goes well with goat's cheese, chicken or fish.

½ teaspoon garlic, crushed

4 tablespoons hazelnut oil

1 tablespoon sherry vinegar

Place all the ingredients in a screw-top jar and shake vigorously. Season with salt and pepper to taste.

Left   Fromage frais and tapenade dressing

TOMATO JUICE DRESSING

This is a proper summer dressing, especially if the tomatoes and herbs come straight from the garden! Serve with rocket (arugula), avocados, tomatoes or chargrilled vegetables.

300ml (10 fl oz/1¼ cups) fresh tomato juice

1 teaspoon tomato purée

4 large leaves fresh basil, chopped

1 teaspoon garlic, crushed

6 tablespoons olive oil

1 tablespoon white wine vinegar

Whisk all the ingredients together in a bowl. Season with salt and pepper to taste.

PARMESAN DRESSING

This popular dressing is delicious served with a fresh green salad and crispy croûtons. Alternatively, try it with smoked chicken or celery.

1 egg, size 2

1 teaspoon garlic, crushed

Juice of 1 lime

1 teaspoon Dijon mustard

10 tablespoons olive oil

8 anchovy fillets , chopped into small pieces

25g (1 oz/2 tablespoons) Parmesan cheese, finely grated

2 tablespoons yoghurt

Whisk the egg with garlic, lime juice and mustard until smooth. Then, one tablespoon at a time, slowly add the olive oil. Stir in the remaining ingredients and season with salt and pepper to taste.

• Croûtons – gently fry one slice of white bread (crusts removed) in olive oil until golden, remove from the pan and cool. Rub both sides of the bread with a clove of fresh garlic and cut into small cubes. Croûtons can be stored in an airtight container for 48 hours, but are best made fresh.

TOASTED SESAME DRESSING

The distinctive taste of sesame will enhance a crisp green salad, artichokes, chicken or prawns (shrimp).

25g (1 oz/2 tablespoons) toasted sesame seeds.

2 tablespoons sesame oil

4 tablespoons olive oil

1 tablespoon white wine vinegar

½ teaspoon grain mustard

Over a low heat, gently fry sesame seeds in sesame oil until golden. Cool, tip into a bowl then whisk in the remaining ingredients and season with salt and pepper to taste.

• This dressing can also be served warm.

ORIENTAL DRESSING

Use this spicy, aromatic dressing to enhance the flavour of prawns (shrimp), chicken, pasta, mangetout (snow peas), corn and crispy vegetable dishes.

3 tablespoons soya sauce

1 teaspoon tabasco sauce

1 teaspoon garlic, crushed

¼ teaspoon muscovado sugar

120ml (4 fl oz/½ cup) olive oil

1 tablespoon sesame oil

3 tablespoons red wine vinegar

½ teaspoon ground black pepper

Whisk all the ingredients together in a bowl or blender until the sugar has dissolved and the consistency is smooth.

Right Parmesan dressing

Chorizo and watercress dressing

ANCHOVY DRESSING

A wonderfully pungent, fish-flavoured dressing; delicious with cheese, roasted aubergines (eggplant), artichokes, fish or a crisp green salad.

8 anchovy fillets
1 teaspoon garlic, crushed
8 tablespoons olive oil
2 tablespoons white wine vinegar
Juice of ½ lemon

Mix all ingredients in a blender until smooth. Season with black pepper.
• If the mixture is too salty, add more lemon juice, a teaspoonful at a time, until the taste is correct.

BLUE CHEESE DRESSING

This all-time favourite is simply bursting with flavour. Serve with iceberg or Cos lettuce, chicken, celery or salmon.

3 tablespoons soured cream or crème fraîche
50g (2 oz/¼ cup) blue cheese, grated
1 shallot, finely grated
1 teaspoon garlic, crushed
2 tablespoons mayonnaise
3 tablespoons olive oil
1 tablespoon white wine vinegar
1 teaspoon Dijon mustard

Put all the ingredients in a blender and mix until smooth. Season with salt and pepper to taste.

CHORIZO AND WATERCRESS DRESSING

This is a wonderful combination, delicious with pork, salami, peppers, iceberg lettuce, watercress, cheese and pasta dishes.

50g (2 oz/¼ cup) thinly sliced chorizo, cut into strips
25g (1 oz/2 tablespoons) watercress leaves
300ml (10 fl oz/1¼ cups) olive oil
2 tablespoons white wine vinegar
Juice of 1 lemon
1 teaspoon Dijon mustard

Place all the ingredients, except the chorizo, in a blender and purée until smooth. Transfer the liquid to a bowl and mix in the chorizo. Season with salt and pepper.
• Best if kept refrigerated for 4–6 hours before serving; this allows the flavour of the sausage to infuse into the dressing.

BLACK OLIVE DRESSING

Use this dark, rich dressing to create a dramatic effect against pale ingredients such as globe artichokes, white fish, crab, scallops or pasta.

1 teaspoon black olive paste

4 tablespoons olive oil

2 tablespoons white wine vinegar

Place all the ingredients in a bowl and whisk until smooth. Season with salt and pepper to taste.

BASIL AND ALMOND DRESSING

This dressing not only smells good but tastes wonderful, too. Perfection with either a green bean, tomato or goat's cheese salad.

1 teaspoon grain mustard

3 tablespoons white wine vinegar

25g (1 oz/1 tablespoon) basil leaves, finely chopped

25g (1 oz/1 tablespoon) toasted almonds, finely chopped

300ml (10 fl oz/1¼ cups) olive oil

Whisk mustard, vinegar, basil and almonds together, then gradually beat in the oil until well blended. Season with salt and pepper.

BALSAMIC VINEGAR AND PISTACHIO DRESSING

This dark, gutsy dressing is scrumptious with a warm chicken liver salad. Alternatively, try it with sweet peppers, onions or goat's cheese.

15g (½ oz/1 tablespoon) pistachio nuts, finely chopped

½ teaspoon garlic, crushed

4 tablespoons walnut oil

3 tablespoons pistachio oil

3 tablespoons balsamic vinegar

Place all the ingredients into a screw-top jar and shake well. Season with salt and pepper.

CREAM CHEESE AND WALNUT DRESSING

Its distinct nutty flavour makes this a wonderful dressing to serve with tomatoes, celery or a crisp green salad.

175ml (6 fl oz/¾ cup) crème fraîche

100g (4 oz/½ cup) cream cheese

25g (1 oz/⅛ cup) walnuts, chopped

1 teaspoon tarragon, chopped

4 tablespoons walnut oil

1 tablespoon lemon juice

½ teaspoon Dijon mustard

Put crème fraîche and cream cheese into a blender and mix together well. Transfer the mixture to a bowl and stir in the rest of the ingredients. Season with salt and pepper to taste.

Aubergine and red pepper salad served with black olive dressing

CHIVE VINAIGRETTE

A delicious summer dressing; excellent with white fish, rice, risotto or a light pasta salad.

50g (2 oz/¼ cup) chives
2 tablespoons white wine vinegar
6 tablespoons olive oil

Finely chop one-third of the chives and set aside. Put remaining chives and vinegar into a blender and whisk to a purée. Strain off the liquid and discard the leftover pulp. Whisk olive oil into the liquid and garnish with the remaining chopped chives just before serving. Season with salt and pepper to taste.

SAFFRON DRESSING

This is a full-flavoured, aromatic dressing; try it with mussels, crab, chicken or pasta.

½ teaspoon saffron threads or powder
1 shallot, very finely chopped
1 teaspoon garlic, crushed
1 tablespoon walnut oil
3 tablespoons olive oil
2 tablespoons white wine vinegar
1 tablespoon Dijon mustard

Place saffron, shallots, garlic and oils in a heavy pan and cook slowly over a low heat until the oil takes on the colour of the saffron. Transfer the mixture to a bowl. When cool, add the remaining ingredients and whisk until smooth.

SMOKED COD'S ROE DRESSING

This is a subtle, creamy dressing with a lovely fishy flavour. Serve with pasta, avocado, aubergines (eggplant) or palm hearts.

25g (1 oz/2 tablespoons) smoked cod's roe, skin removed and sieved
Juice of 1 lime
Peel of 1 lime, grated
½ teaspoon garlic, finely chopped
6 tablespoons olive oil

Mix cod's roe, lime juice and grated peel together until the roe softens. Add the garlic, and, stirring continuously, slowly pour in the oil. Mix all the ingredients together to a smooth consistency. Season with salt and pepper.
•If cod's roe is unavailable use taramasalata.

SUN-DRIED TOMATO DRESSING

Shades of the Med! This colourful dressing is perfection served with goat's cheese, Parma ham, lettuce hearts or pasta.

2 teaspoons sun-dried tomato paste
4 tablespoons olive oil
2 tablespoons white wine vinegar

Whisk all the ingredients together until smooth. Season with salt and pepper.
•To make a stronger, more textured dressing, add 1 teaspoon chopped sun-dried tomatoes cut into thin strips.

TOASTED ALMOND DRESSING

A crunchy, nutty dressing - just the thing to pep up a salad of pork, celery, guinea fowl or cheese.

25g (1oz/2 tablespoons) blanched almonds, toasted and finely chopped
3 tablespoons cider vinegar
2 tablespoons walnut oil
3 tablespoons olive oil

Put all the ingredients in a bowl and whisk together well. Season with salt and pepper to taste.

Right A selection of dry pasta with some of the raw ingredients used to make sun-dried tomato dressing

PESTO DRESSING

This versatile dressing has a wonderful Mediterranean flavour.
Try it with pasta, cheese, Parma ham, salami, salmon or shellfish.

25g (1 oz/2 tablespoons) fresh basil leaves
25g (1 oz/2 tablespoons) pine kernels
25g (1 oz/2 tablespoons) Parmesan cheese
2 teaspoons garlic, crushed
300ml (10 fl oz/1¼ cups) olive oil
Juice of ½ lemon

Place all the ingredients in a liquidiser and blend until smooth. Add
salt and pepper to taste.

CHILLI DRESSING

Try this lightly piquant dressing with chick peas, prawns
(shrimp), chicken or pasta.

1 teaspoon chilli paste
4 tablespoons olive oil
1 tablespoon white wine vinegar
Juice of ½ lemon

Whisk all the ingredients together in a bowl. Season with salt and
pepper to taste.

OYSTER AND SHALLOT DRESSING

Wickedly moreish, this full-bodied dressing is excellent with
bean sprouts, noodles, pasta or seafood.

1½ tablespoons oyster sauce
1 large shallot, finely chopped
2 teaspoons rice vinegar
2 tablespoons sesame oil
2 tablespoons olive oil

Put all the ingredients into a screw-top jar and shake vigorously.
Season with salt and pepper to taste.

GREEN HERB VINAIGRETTE

This dressing has a wonderfully fresh, herby flavour. Perfect
with smoked pork fillet, poached salmon, chicken, pasta, avocados or
tomatoes.

25g (1 oz/2 tablespoons) mixed chervil, dill and basil
1 tablespoon green herb mustard
300ml (10 fl oz/1¼ cups) olive oil
2 tablespoons white wine vinegar
2 tablespoons cold water

Place all the ingredients in a liquidiser and blend until smooth. Season
with salt and pepper to taste.
•If any of the suggested herbs are unavailable, replace with either
chives, fennel or marjoram.

SWEET PEPPER DRESSING

This is a heavenly dressing; excellent with pasta, chicken, salmon
or monkfish.

½ red pepper
½ yellow pepper
1 teaspoon garlic, crushed
50ml (2 fl oz/¼ cup) white wine vinegar
300ml (10 fl oz/1¼ cups) olive oil

Blanch peppers in hot fat until they blister and deepen in colour.
Remove, and when cool, peel and remove seeds and the core. Place
peppers, garlic and vinegar in a liquidiser and blend until smooth.
Transfer the mixture to a bowl and carefully fold in the olive oil.
This dressing looks more attractive if left in its 'separated'
state and not combined as in most of the dressings. Season
with salt and pepper to taste.
• If fresh peppers are not available, buy
those in a tin or jar.

Left Salad of pasta and sweet pepper dressing

CITRUS DRESSING

This dressing is quick, easy to prepare, and simply delicious.
Serve with shellfish, bream, smoked cod's roe and crab.

Grated rind and juice of ½ lemon

Grated rind and juice of ½ lime

Grated rind and juice of ½ orange

½ teaspoon sugar

8 tablespoons olive oil

½ teaspoon salt

Combine all the ingredients in a screw-top jar and shake vigorously to
blend. Season with freshly ground black pepper.

WALNUT DRESSING

This wonderful, nutty dressing is perfection with mackerel,
bream, avocado, chicken or a crisp green salad.

50g (2 oz/¼ cup) walnuts, finely chopped

2 tablespoons walnut oil

2 tablespoons olive oil

2 tablespoons white wine vinegar

1 teaspoon Dijon mustard

Whisk all the ingredients together and season with salt and pepper
to taste.

GREEN OLIVE DRESSING

This dressing has a rich Mediterranean flavour; wonderful
with pasta, squid, artichokes and monkfish.

2 teaspoons green olive paste

15g (½ oz/1 tablespoon) fresh basil, chopped

4 tablespoons olive oil

2 tablespoons white wine vinegar

1 teaspoon Dijon mustard

Whisk all the ingredients together until smooth. Season with salt
and pepper.

Left Salad of squid and herring served with citrus dressing

SHERRY AND CHILLI DRESSING

A hot, spicy dressing which can be served with crab, chicken, pasta or cheese.

1 shallot, finely chopped
1 teaspoon red chilli, seeded and chopped
1 teaspoon garlic, crushed
1 teaspoon soft brown sugar
4 tablespoons walnut oil
4 teaspoons sherry vinegar
¼ teaspoon salt
4 tablespoons olive oil

Put all the ingredients, except the olive oil, in a bowl and mix together. well. Then, whisking continuously, slowly add the olive oil until the mixture is evenly blended.

CHAMPAGNE AND PINE KERNEL DRESSING

This is a light, nutty dressing; delicious with crab, lobster, chicken, salmon or chicory (Belgian endive).

25g (1 oz/2 tablespoons) pine kernels

2 tablespoons champagne vinegar
2 tablespoons olive oil
2 tablespoons walnut oil
1 teaspoon Dijon mustard

Spread pine kernels evenly on a baking tray and place in a pre-heated oven (180°C/350°F/Gas 4) for 3-4 minutes, until golden brown. Remove and cool. Then put all the ingredients into a bowl and mix together well. Season with salt and pepper.
• Best made 4-6 hours before serving so the full flavour of the pine kernels can infuse into the dressing.

CORIANDER AND LIME DRESSING

Bursting with flavour, this delicious dressing is wonderful with chicken, squid, scallops, mangetout (snow peas) and artichoke salads.

25g (1 oz/2 tablespoons) coriander leaves, finely chopped
Juice of 2 small limes
2 tablespoons olive oil
2 tablespoons walnut oil
1 teaspoon Dijon mustard

Whisk all ingredients together until smooth. Season with salt and pepper.

DILL AND YOGHURT DRESSING

A wonderful summer combination; serve with cucumber, salmon, fish or goat's cheese.

25g (1 oz/2 tablespoons) fresh dill, finely chopped
5 tablespoons plain yoghurt
½ teaspoon garlic, crushed
Juice of ½ lemon

Put all the ingredients into a bowl and mix together well. Season with salt and pepper to taste.

THAI DRESSING

Use this exotic oriental dressing to spice up bean shoots, monkfish, mangetout (snow peas) or king prawns (shrimp).

1 tablespoon rice vinegar
1 tablespoon light soya sauce
1½ tablespoons na pla fish sauce
½ teaspoon chilli sauce
1 tablespoon sesame oil
1 teaspoon dark brown sugar

Put all the ingredients in a bowl and whisk together until smooth. Season with salt and pepper to taste.
• If na pla fish sauce is unavailable, substitute with the same quantity of oyster sauce.

Right   Queen scallops covered with sherry and chilli dressing and served on a bed of seaweed

CAPER AND ANCHOVY DRESSING

This tasty, full-bodied dressing is perfection served with fish, a crisp green salad or pasta.

3 egg yolks, hard-boiled
2 tablespoons lemon juice
2 teaspoons Dijon mustard
1 teaspoon garlic, crushed
8 tablespoons olive oil
2 tablespoons capers, chopped
6 anchovy fillets, rinsed, drained and finely chopped

Cream egg yolks and lemon juice thoroughly; then, still beating, add mustard and garlic. Stirring gently, pour the olive oil into the mixture until it begins to thicken; at this point add the capers and anchovies. Season with salt and pepper if necessary.

PIQUANT TOMATO DRESSING

A gusty, strong-flavoured dressing with a lovely, creamy consistency. Try it with prawns (shrimp), salmon or a crisp green salad.

100ml (4fl oz/½ cup) mayonnaise (see basic recipe)
25g (1 oz/2 tablespoons) onion, finely chopped
50g (2 oz/¼ cup) red pepper, seeded and chopped
1 small gherkin (cornichon), finely chopped
½ teaspoon tomato purée
1 tablespoon tomato ketchup
1 tablespoon worcestershire sauce
2 tablespoons brandy

Put all the ingredients in a bowl and mix to a smooth consistency. Season with salt and pepper to taste.

AVOCADO AND CRÈME FRAÎCHE DRESSING

Simple to make, try this wonderful creamy dressing to enhance the subtle flavour of white fish, such as halibut, bass and turbot, as well as chicken and prawns (shrimp).

1 ripe avocado, peeled, stoned and chopped
250ml (9fl oz/1⅛ cup) crème fraîche
1 teaspoon garlic, crushed
2 tablespoons olive oil
1 teaspoon lemon juice

Put all the ingredients in a bowl and mix until smooth. Season with salt and pepper to taste.
• This is a fairly thick dressing. For a thinner, smoother consistency, add 150ml (5fl oz/⅔ cup) water to the mixture and whizz together in a blender.
• To avoid discolouration, store in the fridge in an airtight container for no more than 1½ hours before serving.

WARM CHILLI AND GARLIC DRESSING

A pungent, spicy dressing; serve warm to accentuate the lovely garlicky flavour. Delicious with king prawns (shrimp), pasta or mushrooms.

5 tablespoons olive oil
1 red chilli, seeded and finely chopped
1 teaspoon garlic, crushed
1 shallot, finely chopped
Juice of ½ lemon

Put the olive oil in a heavy pan and gently cook chilli, garlic and shallot until soft. Whisk in the lemon juice and season with salt and pepper. Serve immediately.

Left   Chargrilled halibut on a bed of avocado and crème fraîche dressing

PEANUT DRESSING

An ingenious combination of ingredients blended together to create an exciting nutty dressing. Try the dressing with celery, blue cheese, chicken or fish.

4 tablespoons crunchy peanut butter

1 tablespoon soy sauce

2 tablespoons crème fraîche

1 teaspoon root ginger, finely grated

1 teaspoon garlic, crushed

3 tablespoons groundnut oil

3 tablespoons white wine vinegar

4 tablespoons cold water

Place all the ingredients in a blender and mix until smooth. Season with salt and pepper to taste.

PIQUANT DRESSING

As its name suggests, Piquant Dressing has a distinct spicy flavour. Excellent with game, pigeon or venison.

½ teaspoon tabasco sauce

2 teaspoons soya sauce

1 teaspoon garlic, crushed

2 teaspoons muscovado sugar

175ml (6 fl oz/¾ cup) olive oil

3 tablespoons cider vinegar

½ teaspoon horseradish mustard

¼ teaspoon salt

Put all the ingredients in a bowl or blender and mix together until the sugar dissolves. Season with freshly ground black pepper.

Left Chicken kebabs with peanut dressing

CUMIN AND CORIANDER DRESSING

A robust, spicy dressing; excellent with prawns (shrimp), squid, pasta or chicken.

1 teaspoon garlic, finely chopped

½ teaspoon ground cumin

½ teaspoon ground coriander

2 tablespoons sherry vinegar

4 tablespoons olive oil

Mix garlic, cumin, coriander and vinegar into a paste. Gradually add the oil until the mixture has a smooth consistency.

GRAIN MUSTARD AND HONEY DRESSING

This delicately flavoured dressing has a lovely texture which will enhance a salad of chicken, pasta, cheese or avocado.

2 tablespoons clear honey.

4 tablespoons olive oil

1 tablespoon tarragon vinegar

1 tablespoon grain mustard

Whisk all the ingredients together until smooth. Season with salt and pepper to taste.

YOGHURT AND GINGER DRESSING

A simple, but wonderful dressing where each flavour comes through individually. Delicious with prawns (shrimp), guinea fowl, duck and chicken.

150ml (5fl oz/⅔ cup) thick set natural yoghurt

1 tablespoon clear honey

1 teaspoon crystallized ginger, finely chopped

1 tablespoon lemon juice

¼ teaspoon Dijon mustard

Beat all the ingredients together until creamy and smooth. Season with salt and pepper to taste and serve slightly chilled.

HONEY AND GARLIC DRESSING

The sweet and sour combination of honey and garlic goes beautifully with confit of duck, chicken or pasta.

2 tablespoons clear honey

4 tablespoons lemon juice

½ teaspoon garlic, crushed

3 tablespoons olive oil

Whisk honey, lemon juice and garlic together until well blended. Continue whisking and slowly add the olive oil. Season with salt and pepper to taste.

ALLSPICE AND BITTERS DRESSING

A piquant dressing with a distinct spicy flavour. Wonderful with a salad of pigeon or game.

2 sugar cubes

6 teaspoons Angostura bitters

¼ teaspoon ground allspice

¼ teaspoon coarse grain mustard

4 teaspoons red wine vinegar

5 tablespoons olive oil

Soak the sugar cubes in the Angostura bitters, then whisk together with the allspice, mustard and vinegar. Slowly add the olive oil, whisking gently until the consistency becomes slightly thicker. Season with salt and pepper to taste.

Left Confit of duck with yoghurt and ginger dressing

WARM BLACK CHERRY AND KIRSCH DRESSING

This dark, sophisticated dressing is irresistible! Serve warm with chicken livers, duck or pork.

4 ripe black cherries, stoned
1 tablespoon kirsch
3 tablespoons olive oil
1 tablespoon cherry vinegar

Over a medium heat, warm the cherries and kirsch in a heavy pan until the liquid takes on the colour of the cherries. Remove from the heat, mix in the olive oil and vinegar and season with salt and pepper. If necessary warm through gently. Serve immediately.

WARM CHILLI AND RASPBERRY DRESSING

An exotic combination of chilli and raspberry is the inspiration behind this colourful dressing. Delicious with scallops, lentils or squid.

4 fresh ripe raspberries
½ red chilli, seeded and finely sliced
½ teaspoon chilli paste
½ teaspoon garlic, crushed
3 tablespoons olive oil
1 tablespoon raspberry vinegar

Place all the ingredients in a pan and warm through gently over a low heat until the raspberries start to break up and colour the liquid. Transfer the mixture to a bowl, whisk together well, season with salt and pepper and serve.

BALSAMIC AND RAISIN DRESSING

A slightly tart dressing; just the thing to pep up a duck or chicken liver salad.

25g (1 oz/2 tablespoons) raisins
4 tablespoons balsamic vinegar
½ teaspoon garlic, crushed
6 tablespoons olive oil
1 teaspoon Dijon mustard

Put raisins and balsamic vinegar in a bowl and leave to soak for 24 hours. Then add the remaining ingredients and whisk into a smooth consistency. Season with salt and pepper to taste.

LIME PICKLE DRESSING

Try this refreshing, slightly tangy dressing with goose, duck or guinea fowl.

2 teaspoons lime pickle, finely chopped
1 tablespoon lime juice
4 tablespoons olive oil

Place all the ingredients in a bowl and whisk into a smooth consistency. Season with salt and pepper to taste.

BEETROOT AND WALNUT DRESSING

This colourful dressing looks and tastes wonderful served with crab, game, pigeon, venison or cauliflower.

1 medium beetroot (75g/3oz/⅓ cup), cooked and finely grated
1 teaspoon Dijon mustard
1 tablespoon sherry vinegar
3 tablespoons walnut oil

Mix grated beetroot with mustard and vinegar. Gradually stir in the oil and season with salt and pepper to taste.

Right A selection of raw ingredients used to make beetroot and walnut dressing

CARAWAY AND SMOKED BACON DRESSING

This dressing not only smells good, but tastes wonderful too! Serve warm with either pork, goat's cheese, peppers or aubergines (eggplant).

4 tablespoons olive oil

75g (3 oz/⅓ cup) smoked streaky bacon, cut into fine strips

1 shallot, finely chopped

1 teaspoon garlic, crushed

1 teaspoon caraway seeds

2 tablespoons red wine vinegar

2 tablespoons walnut oil

Put olive oil and bacon in a heavy pan and fry until the bacon is crispy. Add shallots, garlic and caraway seeds and heat for another minute. Transfer the mixture to a bowl, whisk in the vinegar and walnut oil and serve.

• This dressing can also be served cold.

REDCURRANT AND MINT DRESSING

A slightly sweet, minty dressing which is delicious served with lamb, potatoes, avocado or courgettes.

1 tablespoon redcurrant jelly

2 tablespoons red wine vinegar

4 tablespoons olive oil

15g (½ oz/1 tablespoon) mint leaves, finely chopped

Put the jelly and vinegar into a heavy saucepan and warm over a low heat until the jelly has dissolved. Transfer the mixture to a bowl and allow to cool. Then add the olive oil and whisk to a smooth consistency. Add the freshly chopped mint and season with salt and pepper.

Left Fried bacon used for caraway and smoked bacon dressing

ENGLISH MUSTARD DRESSING

This is a wonderful, strong-flavoured dressing; use it to spice up a salad of beef, salmon, leeks, cheese, avocado or tomatoes.

1 teaspoon English mustard

4 tablespoons olive oil

1 tablespoon white wine vinegar

Whisk all the ingredients together until the consistency is smooth. Season with salt and pepper.

GREEN PEPPERCORN AND THYME DRESSING

A piquant dressing with a strong herby flavour. Just the thing to complement beetroot, venison, game, goat's cheese or smoked chicken.

10 green peppercorns, tinned or in a jar

½ teaspoon thyme leaves, finely chopped

6 tablespoons olive oil

2 tablespoons white wine vinegar

1 teaspoon Dijon mustard

Put all the ingredients in a blender and mix until the consistency is smooth. Season with salt and pepper to taste.

GREEN HERB DRESSING

This light, herb-flavoured dressing is delicious with beef, venison, goat's cheese, pasta or fish.

1 tablespoon green herb mustard

4 tablespoons olive oil

1 tablespoon white wine vinegar

Put all the ingredients in a screw-top jar and shake vigorously until well blended. Season with salt and pepper to taste.

ORANGE AND SHALLOT DRESSING

A wonderful light, tangy dressing; perfection with pork spare ribs, chicken, turkey, guinea fowl, pasta, chicory (Belgian endive) or watercress.

Rind of 1 orange, finely grated

Juice of 1 orange.

1 shallot, finely chopped

6 tablespoons olive oil

1 tablespoon white wine vinegar

1 tablespoons grain mustard

Put all the ingredients in a screw-top jar and shake together well. Season with salt and pepper to taste.

RED ONION AND CAPER DRESSING

This is a richly satisfying dressing with a slightly tart edge to it. Serve warm with beef, veal and fish.

5 tablespoons olive oil

½ small red onion, finely diced

½ teaspoon garlic, chopped

1 teaspoon capers

1 teaspoon caper vinegar (use the liquid in which the capers were preserved)

Heat 1 tablespoon of olive oil in a heavy pan and gently sweat the onion and garlic until soft but not browned. Remove pan from the heat and whisk in the rest of the oil and the remaining ingredients. Season with salt and pepper and serve warm.

Right Roasted spare ribs covered with orange and shallot dressing

BLUEBERRY DRESSING

This wonderful fruity dressing is perfection with lamb. Alternatively, use it to enhance other subtle flavours such as chicken, avocado and asparagus.

2 tablespoons fresh blueberries

1 teaspoon sugar

4 tablespoons olive oil

1 tablespoon lemon juice

Put all the ingredients in a blender and mix until smooth. Season with salt and pepper to taste.

ROSEMARY AND CRANBERRY DRESSING

An inspirational dressing with an exquisite, pungent flavour. Delicious with lamb, roasted peppers and aubergines (eggplant).

1 sprig rosemary, finely chopped

2 teaspoons cranberry jelly

1 tablespoon rosemary or redcurrant vinegar

4 tablespoons olive oil

In a thick saucepan heat the rosemary, cranberry jelly and vinegar until the jelly has dissolved. Remove from heat and when cool gradually whisk in the olive oil. Season with salt and pepper.
• This dressing can be served warm.
• As an alternative, use redcurrant jelly.

HORSERADISH DRESSING

A slightly tart, creamy dressing, just the thing to spice up a salad of beef, salmon or pasta.

1 tablespoon horseradish relish

2 tablespoons plain yoghurt

Juice of ½ lemon

Put all the ingredients in a bowl and whisk together well. Season with salt and pepper to taste.

CIDER AND APPLE DRESSING

The subtle combination of sweet and sour is wonderful with pork, duck, smoked goose or guinea fowl.

1 small eating apple, peeled, cored and grated

4 tablespoons olive oil

2 tablespoons cider vinegar

1 teaspoon grain mustard

Put all the ingredients in a screw-top jar and shake together well. Season with salt and pepper to taste.

CURRY DRESSING

There's nothing like a good curry dressing to spice up delicately flavoured meats such as chicken and pork. Excellent with seafood and pasta.

2 teaspoons sultanas, finely chopped

½ teaspoon curry powder

½ teaspoon turmeric

¼ teaspoon powdered ginger

½ shallot, finely chopped

½ teaspoon garlic, crushed

6 tablespoons olive oil

2 tablespoons white wine vinegar

1 teaspoon Dijon mustard

Put all the ingredients in a bowl and whisk together well.

SORREL AND BLACK GRAPE DRESSING

This tangy, aromatic dressing is a delicious mixture of sweet and sour ingredients. Perfect with pork, boiled ham and fish.

25g (1oz/2 tablespoons) sorrel, finely chopped

50g (2oz/¼ cup) small, seedless black grapes, skins removed

1 tablespoon white wine vinegar

1 teaspoon garlic, finely chopped

5 tablespoons olive oil

2 tablespoons natural yoghurt

Place all the ingredients in a bowl and mix together well - this dressing should have a separated appearance. Season with salt and pepper to taste.

POPPY SEED DRESSING

Bursting with flavour, Poppy Seed Dressing is simply delicious served with shellfish, avocados, goat's cheese or mangos.

1 tablespoon poppy seeds
1 tablespoon clear honey
4 tablespoons olive oil
Juice of 1 lime

Put all the ingredients into a bowl and whisk together well. Season with salt and pepper to taste.
• When serving this dressing with sweet dishes, omit the salt and pepper and season with sugar if necessary.

EXOTIC FRUIT DRESSING

This exquisite dressing can be used with either sweet or savoury dishes, so try it with fruit salad, shellfish or poultry.

3 tablespoons fresh mango juice
2 passionfruit, cut in half and the flesh spooned out
1 teaspoon root ginger, finely grated
6 fresh mint leaves, finely chopped
4 tablespoons pistachio oil
1 tablespoon redcurrant vinegar

Place all the ingredients in a bowl and whisk together well.
• If fresh mango is unavailable, use juice from a tin or a carton instead.

LEMON AND THYME DRESSING

This fresh, herby dressing is bursting with flavour. Try it with chicken, globe artichokes, eggs or pasta.

300ml (10fl oz/1¼ cups) olive oil
Juice and grated zest of 2 lemons
1 teaspoon fresh thyme, finely chopped
1 teaspoon shallot, finely chopped
1 teaspoon garlic, finely chopped

Put all the ingredients in a screw-top jar and shake together well. Season with salt and pepper to taste.

Right   A selection of fruits to serve with exotic fruit dressing

ELDERFLOWER DRESSING

This ambrosial dressing is to die for. Serve with melon, mango, or a salad of exotic fruits. Delicious with crab and oysters, too.

4 tablespoons elderflower cordial
4 tablespoons olive oil
1 tablespoon white wine vinegar

Place all the ingredients in a screw-top jar and shake vigorously.
• For a thinner consistency, whisk all the ingredients in a bowl until they start to emulsify, then stop whisking immediately or the mixture will start to thicken again.

LAVENDER DRESSING

A delicately scented dressing; out of this world with melon or poached peaches.

Three 2.5cm (4 in) sprigs lavender, in flower
8 tablespoons water
Juice of ½ lemon
1 tablespoon castor sugar
5 tablespoons olive oil

Remove flowers from the stems and place the flowers in a thick-bottomed pan over a low heat with the water, lemon juice and sugar for about 10-15 minutes (any longer and the flavour may become bitter). Remove from the heat and strain. Cool and whisk in the olive oil.

PASSIONFRUIT AND LEMON BALM DRESSING

Light in texture and full of flavour, this versatile dressing goes beautifully with strawberries and melon or chicken and fish.

4 large, ripe passionfruit, cut in half and flesh and pips spooned out
4 large leaves lemon balm, finely chopped
1 teaspoon light brown sugar
2 tablespoons pistachio oil
2 tablespoons olive oil

Put all the ingredients in a bowl and mix together well.

APRICOT AND ALMOND DRESSING

A colourful, fruity dressing; wonderful served with fresh fruit salad, pineapple, melon or avocado.

25g (1 oz/2 tablespoons) toasted flaked almonds
4 tablespoons crème fraîche
4 tablespoons orange juice
8 tablespoons cold water
50g (2 oz/¼ cup) dried no-soak apricots, chopped

Place all the ingredients, except the apricots, in a blender and mix until smooth. Add the chopped apricots to create a lovely crunchy texture.
• Cold water is used to enhance the cool, fresh taste of the dressing.

BLOOD ORANGE AND CLOVE DRESSING

An exquisitely fresh, clean-tasting dressing with a spicy edge to it. Wonderful with melon, fruit salad or exotic fruits such as mango and pawpaw.

600ml (1 pint/1½ cups) fresh blood orange juice
2 whole cloves, crushed
1 teaspoon demerara sugar
3 tablespoons olive oil
Juice of ½ lime

Reduce the orange juice, sugar and cloves in a heavy pan over a medium heat until approximately 150ml (5fl oz/⅔ cup) of syrupy liquid remains. Transfer the mixture to a bowl, and when cool, mix in the olive oil and lime juice.

Right Poached peaches with lavender dressing

WOODBRIDGE TOWN LIBRARY
10 NEWTON ROAD
WOODBRIDGE, CONN. 06525